A BOOK OF

SEA CREATURES

A   B O O K   O F

SEA CREATURES

INTRODUCTION BY GILL SAUNDERS

VICTORIA AND ALBERT MUSEUM

INTRODUCTION

GILL SAUNDERS

The land has been tamed. Only the sea remains as our last wilderness. In its vast depths may yet lurk monsters and mysteries. An alien hostile element, it has spawned a variety of mythical creatures which embody its dangers, its violent changes of mood, its cruel and arbitrary powers of seduction, illusion and death. Early Hebrew belief allotted each element its own monster: Behemoth on land, Ziz in the air, Leviathan – a serpent unimaginably huge, solitary, immortal – in the sea. In Scandinavian myth the Kraken sleeps in the depths, awaiting the end of the world. Maps and charts from the 16th century and earlier show the seas populated by all manner of outlandish and fantastic creatures which menace the ships and dwarf the islands.

The terrors of the sea were denied by viewing it as a mirror of our world, peopled with sunken cities such as Atlantis. What walked on land had a counterpart in the sea: thus the sea-horse, originally the mythical hippocampus, a creature with the head and forelegs of a horse and the tail of a fish, which draws the chariot of the sea-god Poseidon and his consort Amphitrite; and sea-elephants, sea-

unicorns and sea-lions, a creature depicted in the Oxburgh hangings as a cat with webbed feet and scales instead of fur. The sea-monk was a fantastic figure who appears independently in Chinese and in Scandinavian folklore. The Chinese version is malevolent, capsizing junks. These drowned spirits retained something of their human shape, forever doomed to drift in the sea, unless they could drown another to take their place. Belief in the sea-monk persisted into the 18th century in Europe; the reality was probably a dugong or seal.

There is a similarly prosaic explanation for the mermaid. Indeed some myths combine the real seal with the fantasy of the mermaid. Many cultures, including the Japanese, record the story of a seal – or swan-woman who comes ashore and casts off her skin to become human and dance; if anyone hides her skin she is condemned to remain on land until she can recover it. One such legend is that of the selkies of Ireland and the Scottish isles who are made captive as wives and mothers by such means, but always yearn for their home in the sea. The mermaid may exchange the sea for the land but she always suffers to do so; Hans Christian Andersen's Little Mermaid, who leaves the sea for love of a human prince, sacrifices the power of speech and her every step is acutely painful. A mermaid's beauty is seductive but it is her singing which lures sailors to their doom.

In Greek myth, Poseidon rules the sea, but in earlier beliefs it is identified with the Great Mother, the fish-goddess. The myth in which the goddess devours and then disgorges the Father/Son has a Christian counterpart in the story of Jonah. Swallowed by a 'great fish' (not specifically a whale) Jonah survives in its belly or 'womb', to be reborn, thus prefiguring the death and resurrection of Christ. The dolphin too is a type of Christ, saviour of the ship-wrecked and bearer of souls across the waters. In classical myth, associated with Aphrodite and Eros, or their Roman equivalents, Venus and Cupid, it represents love.

The symbol of the Great Mother or fish-goddess is the pointed-oval, the yoni, which represents both fish and vulva. So pervasive and revered was this symbol, the *'vesica piscis'*, that Christian

DOLPHIN, PROBABLY
INTENDED AS A PAPERWEIGHT.
ENGLISH, BOW, *C.* 1760.
HEIGHT 121MM. SCH.59

evangelists used it as a Christ-symbol, carefully purged of its association with the female genitals. In Christian art it may appear as a sign of the womb, but the older meanings persisted: the yoni is used as a decorative border on Thomas Toft's slipware dish depicting a mermaid, herself a debased form of the great fish-goddess.

As the Ocean, the Great Mother is the source of life. Sea-creatures are thus often symbols of fertility: for instance, the octopus is held to be magical and sacred because it has eight tentacles, eight being the number of fertility in Mediterranean myth. In Christianity too eight is the number of regeneration and rebirth, hence the font ('*piscina*', literally fish-pond) where baptism, or re-birth, is enacted, is usually octagonal.

Several sea-creatures appear amongst the signs of the zodiac: Pisces (the Fishes), Capricorn (the Sea-Goat), and Cancer (the Crab). The sign of the Crab was associated with water, and with the Moon, another of the symbols identified most closely with the Great Mother. The Moon represents the dark side of Nature, the unseen and irrational; it controls the rains and the tides. Amongst the precious stones, the pearl, product of the sea, is emblematic of the Moon. The Triton-figure of the Canning Jewel has a torso of pearl. Given the symbolic meanings of the pearl, the jewel may be seen as a badge of chastity and purity, though Triton himself was generally characterised as lascivious.

Corals and shells formed an important part of 'cabinets of curiosities', those exotic 17th century collections. Shells in particular were highly valued. Perhaps the most beautiful and coveted of shells was the 'Nautilus pompilius', remarkable for its symmetry. The finest examples were mounted in silver, and lidded, to create an elaborate chalice, for ornament rather than use. The mount often depicted a sea theme and the shell itself engraved with fish and other sea-creatures.

Fishes themselves were both decorative and symbolic. Jewellers in particular have exploited their decorative potential:

where Lalique used gold and enamel to create a convincing simulacrum, Simon Costin used the preserved head of a real fish endowed with a jewelled glass eye. Like Turner's Gurnard, a fish out of water, it plays with ideas of sight, perception and context, making of a natural object something artificial.

KOZUKA (KNIFE HANDLE)

MADE FROM BASE METAL WITH

THREE GOLD FISHES.

JAPANESE C.1800. LENGTH

98MM. M1414–1931

SCABBARD FOR A DAGGER

OF LACQUERED WOOD,

RAY FISH SKIN AND BALEEN,

JAPANESE, ABOUT 1850.

565MM. M1335–1926

EARTHENWARE TUREEN
WITH HANDLES IN THE FORM
OF FISHES. GERMAN, FULDA,
C. 1741–43. HEIGHT 248MM
C133&A–1951

PORCELAIN CANE HANDLE
AS A MERMAID. FRENCH,
ST CLOUD, SECOND QUARTER
OF THE 18TH CENTURY.
149MM C446–1909

DISH OF PLIQUE-A-JOUR

ENAMEL. FRENCH,

C. 1905. DIAMETER 283MM.

M24–1972

CELADON PORCELAIN

DISH DECORATED IN UNGLAZED

BROWN 'BISCUIT'.

CHINESE, 14TH CENTURY.

DIAMETER 314MM. C1-1940

STONEWARE VASE WITH
HANDLES IN THE FORM OF
GROTESQUE CREATURES.
BY C.H. BRANNAN, ENGLISH,
C. 1907. HEIGHT 272MM.
CIRC 55–1966

EARTHENWARE FLASK
MOULDED IN THE FORM OF
TWO FISH. CHINESE,
618–906 AD. HEIGHT 244MM.
C88–1939

BOX FOR WRITING
PAPER AND BOX FOR WRITING
UTENSILS. WOOD COVERED
IN WOVEN BAMBOO DECORATED
WITH LACQUER, ENAMELLED
POTTERY AND HORN, JAPANESE,
LATE 17TH CENTURY,
102×381×267MM. W56 AND
W57–1922

IVORY NETSUKE OF AN

OCTOPUS. JAPANESE, 19TH

CENTURY. HEIGHT 28MM.

A397–1904

BOXWOOD AND IVORY NETSUKE

IN THE FORM OF AN

OCTOPUS TRAP. JAPANESE, 19TH

CENTURY. 38MM. A55–1919

EARTHENWARE PLATE
DECORATED WITH
A MERMAID. ENGLISH, MADE
BY THOMAS TOFT, LATE
17TH CENTURY. DIAMETER
438MM. C299–1869

THE BURGHLEY NEF,
MADE FROM A NAUTILUS SHELL
AND MOUNTED IN SILVER
AND PARCEL GILT. IN FRONT
OF THE MAIN MAST OF
THIS SALT-CELLAR ARE THE
LEGENDARY CHARACTERS,
TRISTRAM AND ISEULT.
FRENCH (PARIS) C. 1528.
HEIGHT 346MM. M60–1959

EARTHENWARE GROUP OF

VENUS, CUPID AND A DOLPHIN,

ENGLISH, STAFFORDSHIRE,

EARLY 19TH CENTURY.

HEIGHT 241MM. C116–1874

MAIOLICA PLATE ENAMELLED
WITH MARINE DEITIES.
ITALIAN, MADE IN URBINO OR
RESARO, *C.* 1540–45.
DIAMETER 264MM. C1704–1855

WOODEN NETSUKE

OF A MERMAID ON A CLAM.

JAPANESE, 18TH CENTURY.

50MM. A52–1952

EARTHENWARE BOWL WITH

LUSTRE DECORATION,

SPANISH (VALENCIA), FIRST

HALF OF THE 15TH

CENTURY. DIAMETER 508MM

C486–1864

EARTHENWARE PLATE WITH

LUSTRE DECORATION.

ENGLISH, MADE AT WILLIAM

DE MORGAN'S FACTORY,

1898–1907. DIAMETER 239MM

C421–1919

EARTHENWARE BOWL

DECORATED WITH LUSTRE.

ENGLISH, MADE BY

CARTER & CO OF POOLE AND

DECORATED BY WILLIAM

DE MORGAN, 1904, OUTSIDE

WITH 3 FISHES AND

INSIDE WITH 5 FISHES.

DIAMETER 184MM

C859–1905

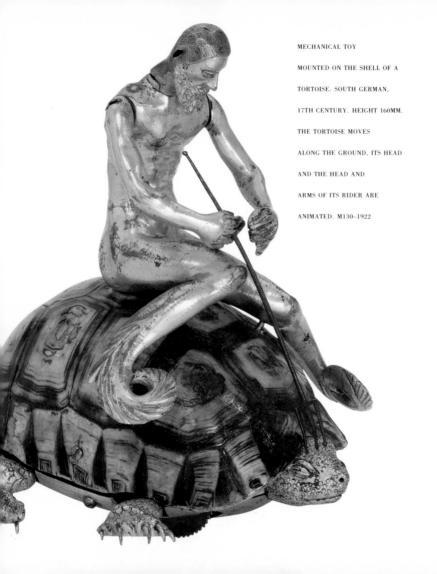

MECHANICAL TOY
MOUNTED ON THE SHELL OF A
TORTOISE. SOUTH GERMAN,
17TH CENTURY. HEIGHT 160MM.
THE TORTOISE MOVES
ALONG THE GROUND, ITS HEAD
AND THE HEAD AND
ARMS OF ITS RIDER ARE
ANIMATED. M130–1922

A NYMPH SEATED ON THE BACK
OF A SEA-MONSTER BY
ANDREA BRIOSCO. ITALIAN,
MADE IN PADUA, EARLY
16TH CENTURY. HEIGHT 220MM.

A91–1910

BROOCH. GOLD COLOURED,

ENRICHED WITH ENAMELS AND

SET WITH TWO FIRE

OPALS. FRENCH, MADE BY

LALIQUE IN THE EARLY

20TH CENTURY. HEIGHT 30MM

M520–1924

BROOCH, MADE OF THE

CONSERVED HEAD OF A BREAM

WITH A GLASS EYE.

COMMISSIONED BY THE MUSEUM.

ENGLISH, MADE BY SIMON

COSTIN, 1988. HEIGHT 79MM

M61–1988

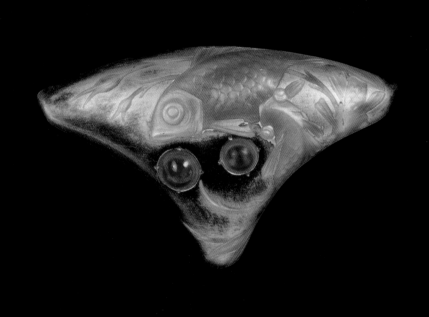

EARTHENWARE DRUG

POT, ENAMELLED WITH SEA

CREATURES. ITALIAN,

CASTEL DURANTE,

C. 1550–60. HEIGHT 330MM

C2590–1856

IVORY NETSUKE OF THE

TREASURE SHIP WITH THE SEVEN

LUCKY GODS ON BOARD.

JAPANESE, 19TH CENTURY.

HEIGHT 57MM. A746–1910

PUBLISHED BY

THE VICTORIA AND ALBERT MUSEUM 1992

© THE TRUSTEES OF THE VICTORIA AND ALBERT MUSEUM

DESIGNED BY BERNARD HIGTON

DESIGN ASSOCIATE: BRIGITTE HALLIDAY

PICTURE RESEARCH BY SIMON BLAIN

SERIES DEVISED BY JENNIFER BLAIN AND LESLEY BURTON

PRINTED IN SINGAPORE

ISBN 1 85177 111 5